A to Z England

BY BYRON AND REBECCA AUGUSTIN

children's press

A Division of Scholastic Inc.
New York Toronto London Auckland Sydney
Mexico City New Delhi Hong Kong
Danbury, Connecticut

Consultant: David Campion, Assistant Professor of History, Lewis and Clark College
Series Design: Marie O'Neill
Photo Research: Caroline Anderson

The photos on the cover show a red fox (top left), Big Ben (top right), a crown from the Crown Jewels (bottom right), and a young boy dressed as a "bobby" (bottom center).

Photographs © 2005: AP/Wide World Photos: 28 bottom (Alberto Martin/EFE), 12 top (Phil Noble/Pool); Art Resource, NY/Victoria & Albert Museum, London: 33; Corbis Images: 27 right (Archivo Iconografico, S.A.), 7 right (David Ball), 15 bottom (Bettmann), 37 bottom (Adrian Carroll/Eye Ubiquitous), 12 bottom (Mike Finn-Kelcey/Reuters), 32 (Franz-Marc Frei), 26 (Colin Garratt/Milepost 92 1/2), 17 left, 24 (Tim Graham/Sygma), 13, 37 top (Hulton-Deutsch Collection), 35 bottom (Bob Krist), 5 bottom (George McCarthy), 25 bottom (Christine Osborne), cover bottom right (PoodlesRock), 6 top (Premium Stock), 6 bottom (Augustus Welby Pugin/Royalty-Free), 8 (Ariel Skelley), 9 top (Peter Turnley), 25 top (Patrick Ward), 16 (Nik Wheeler), 35 top (Adam Woolfitt); Getty Images: 19 (Jon Arnold/Taxi), cover top left (Tom Tietz/Stone); Minden Pictures/Jim Brandenburg: 4; Nature Picture Library Ltd./Colin Varndell: 5 top; PictureQuest/Creatas: cover top right; Reuters: 27 left (Pool), 23 (Ian Waldie); Superstock, Inc.: 7 left (age fotostock), 10, 17 right (Peter Harholdt), 11 (Sucre Sale); The Art Archive/Picture Desk/Dagli Orti/Musée du Château de Versailles: 14; TRIP Photo Library: 22 (Robert Belbin), 34 bottom (Roger Cracknell), 34 top (Brian Gibbs), 18 (A. Lambert), 38 (Norman Price), 21, 28 top, 29 (H. Rogers), 36 (Helene Rogers), cover center bottom (Howard Sayer), 9 bottom (Adina Tovy), 31 (B. Turner), 30 (Terry Why), 15 top (Chris Wormald).
Map on page 20 by XNR Productions, Inc.

Library of Congress Cataloging-in-Publication Data
Augustin, Byron.
   England / by Byron Augustin and Rebecca A. Augustin.
      p. cm. — (A to Z)
   Includes bibliographical references and index.
   ISBN 0-516-23653-9 (lib. bdg.)   0-516-24952-5 (pbk.)
   1. England—Juvenile literature. I. Augustin, Rebecca A. II. Title. III. Series.
   DA27.5.A94 2005
   942—dc22   2005006997

1 2 3 4 5 6 7 8 9 10 R 14 13 12 11 10 09 08 07 06 05

Contents

Majestic red deer roam in England's parks and nature preserves.

Animals

England is a small country with a large human population. As a result, most wild animals are found in protected public parks or private **reserves.**

England recently banned fox-hunting.

Deer are the largest mammals found in the wild in England. They have no natural **predators,** and their numbers are growing. This is a problem because they cause traffic accidents and eat crops.

The red fox is a favorite throughout England. It is a very **cunning** animal and is difficult to catch. It will eat almost anything but prefers rodents, birds, and rabbits.

Rabbits are common in England. British author Beatrix Potter wrote a beloved series of children's books about Peter Rabbit and his friends.

Buildings

Buckingham Palace is the official London residence of Queen Elizabeth II.

Lift

means "elevator."

In London, residents and tourists alike can set their clocks by Big Ben's familiar chime.

Buckingham Palace is one of the most famous buildings in the world. It is the home and office for the **monarch** of England. The building has six hundred rooms and many beautiful gardens.

Parliament meets in the Palace of Westminster. The building's best-known feature is its clock tower, Big Ben. Big Ben is actually the nickname for the 13.5-ton bell located in the tower.

The Tower Bridge spans the Thames River as it flows through London.

A distinctive double-decker bus runs past Harrod's, the famous London department store on Brompton Road.

Cities

London is one of the most well-known and historic cities in the world. The city can trace its beginnings back more than two thousand years. More than 7 million people live in London!

The city is located along the banks of the Thames River, which empties into the North Sea. This connection helps make London a busy port and trade center. Manufacturing and banking are also important to the city. London is home to many outstanding museums, theaters, and parks.

Wool keeps both lambs and children warm in England's cold, damp winters.

Dress

In general, the English people dress conservatively. During the summers, cotton clothing is a favorite choice. Wool clothing is popular during the damp, cool winters.

8

English businessmen usually wear suits to work. Older women wear longer skirts and dresses, while younger women often prefer miniskirts. As in many parts of the Western world, younger people in general dress more casually.

The uniforms of members of the Queen's Guard are magnificent. The **tunics** are bright scarlet, with dark blue collars. The pants are dark blue with a red stripe. Most impressive are the black bearskin hats worn by the Guards. The hats are 18 inches (46 centimeters) tall!

These London businessmen are dressed for success.

The guards at Buckingham Palace are recognizable the world around.

9

Exports

English wool has been a valuable export for hundreds of years. England has long been known for the high quality of its specially bred sheep.

England also exports cars such as Land Rovers and Rolls-Royces. Land Rovers were originally developed as farm vehicles, but today are sold all over the world as durable and stylish four-wheel-drive vehicles. Luxurious Rolls-Royces are famous as symbols of wealth and prestige.

Cadbury chocolate candy is also sold all over the world. The chocolate is noted for its creamy texture and delicious taste.

This 1950s Rolls-Royce is a classic.

English Toffee Recipe

WHAT YOU NEED:

- 1 cup finely chopped pecans
- 1 large milk-chocolate candy bar, grated
- 1 pound (4 sticks) butter
- 1 1/2 cups sugar
- 1 cup water
- 1/4 cup white corn syrup

HOW TO MAKE IT:

Butter a cookie sheet, cover with half of the chopped pecans and grated chocolate, and set aside. Combine butter, sugar, water, and syrup in a heavy pan, and bring to a boil while stirring. Test the toffee by spooning a few drops into a cup of cold water. The toffee is done when it hardens into a crisp ball in the cold water. Pour the liquid on the prepared cookie sheet, and cover with the remaining chopped pecans and grated chocolate. Let it cool. Break into pieces when cold. This recipe takes about an hour to prepare and makes twenty-four servings.

Food

The English are known for hearty meals such as roast beef, Yorkshire pudding, and apple pie with cream. Toffee is another favorite sweet. Ask an adult to help you make this recipe.

Queen Elizabeth II has been England's head of state since 1953.

Government

Prime Minister Tony Blair

England's government is a **constitutional monarchy.** The official head of state is Queen Elizabeth II. The Queen is the symbol of leadership. But most political decisions are made by the Parliament.

The Parliament is composed of the House of Lords and the House of Commons. Members of the House of Lords are appointed or elected by other lords, or they inherit their positions. Members of the House of Commons are democratically elected. Parliament is led by a prime minister, who is the leader of the majority party in the House of Commons.

Whole neighborhoods in London were destroyed during bombing raids in World War II.

History

One of the most significant events in English history began during World War II (1939–1945). On September 7, 1940, Adolf Hitler, dictator of Nazi Germany, ordered a **blitz** on London. For fifty-seven consecutive nights, hundreds of bombs fell on London. Many people were killed and the city was badly damaged. Ordinary people showed their courage by continuing their everyday lives in spite of the terrible destruction.

The British Royal Air Force fought back bravely. Prime Minister Winston Churchill praised the British fighter pilots with this famous quote: "Never in the field of human conflict has so much been owed by so many to so few." England did not surrender and was among the countries that won the war.

Poet and playwright **William Shakespeare** lived during the reign of England's Queen Elizabeth I.

Important People

William Shakespeare and the Beatles
are names recognized around the world.
They represent some of England's greatest
contributions to Western culture.

Shakespeare was born in the town of Stratford-upon-Avon. Today, Stratford is home to the Royal Shakespeare Company and is a popular tourist destination.

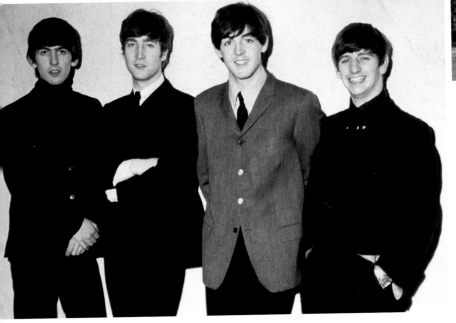

Meet the Beatles! George Harrison, John Lennon, Paul McCartney, and Ringo Starr changed popular music forever in the early 1960s.

Shakespeare was born in Stratford-upon-Avon in 1564. Many people believe that he was the greatest playwright and poet of all time. His plays are still performed regularly in theaters around the world. Some of his best-known plays include *Hamlet, Romeo and Juliet,* and *The Merchant of Venice.*

The Beatles remain the most popular musical group in history. They began their careers in the city of Liverpool. Band members John Lennon, Paul McCartney, George Harrison, and Ringo Starr changed Western music forever.

In England, a police officer is sometimes called a "bobby."

Jobs

England has been an important manufacturing center since the Industrial Revolution began there in the 1700s. Today, however, almost three out of four workers are employed in service jobs.

England's most important service jobs are in banking, insurance, stock markets, and real estate. Other jobs are in education, health care, and tourism.

Keepsakes

Wedgwood china is recognized as one of the world's most elegant table settings. Josiah Wedgwood founded his company in 1759. He was named "Potter to Her Majesty" by Queen Charlotte in 1765.

Wedgwood china has graced the tables of kings and presidents around the world. For many families, Wedgwood china is a family **heirloom.**

Wedgwood china is fit for royalty. Prince Phillip (husband to Queen Elizabeth II), examines a piece of Wedgwood.

Wedgwood has been known for its quality and beauty for nearly 250 years.

People have lived in and around picturesque
Buckden Village for some 1,000 years.

Land

Mountains, **moors,** and rolling hills shape
the landscape of England. Sparkling
streams and glimmering lakes highlight
the countryside.

Like the White Cliffs of Dover, the Seven Sisters Cliffs along the Strait of Dover between England and France are made of chalk.

The Pennines are known as "the backbone of England." They are a low mountain range that passes through the central part of the country. The Lake District in northwest England is stunningly beautiful. It contains the country's highest peak, largest lake, and breathtaking waterfalls.

The chalk cliffs along the Sussex coast and further east to Dover are among the world's best-known landmarks. They are the first feature visitors see when crossing the English Channel from France.

ENGLAND

Map

ATLANTIC
OCEAN

Scotland

*North
Sea*

UNITED

Northern
Ireland

KINGDOM

Prime Meridian

THE PENNINES

Liverpool

IRELAND

England

Stratford-
upon-Avon

Wales

London

Thames River

Stonehenge

Dover

English Channel

N
W ◄ ● ► E
S

MILES
0   100
KILOMETERS
0   100

20

Nation

England is one of four countries that make up the United Kingdom. The other three countries are Scotland, Wales, and Northern Ireland.

The flag of England represents Saint George. Saint George is the patron saint of England. His emblem was a red cross on a white background. The emblem was introduced as England's flag in 1194 by King Richard the Lionheart. The cross is now the center of the Union Jack flag, which is the flag for all of the United Kingdom (below).

Tennis champion Pete Sampras held his trophy high after he won the men's final at Wimbledon.

Only in England

The Wimbledon Lawn Tennis Championships make up the most famous tennis tournament in the world.

Tennis players everywhere dream of playing at Wimbledon's Centre Court.

The tournament is held during the end of June and the beginning of July. More than 500,000 spectators attend the matches. Millions of viewers around the world watch the events on television.

The final matches take place at Centre Court, a stadium that seats 13,500 fans. Some of the great men's champions include Bjorn Borg, Rod Laver, and Pete Sampras. Margaret Court, Billie Jean King, and Martina Navratilova are famous women's champions.

These students at Eton College are celebrating their school's five hundredth anniversary!

People

Flat
means "apartment."

Almost 90 percent of England's population is Caucasian. Most Caucasians are **descendants** of Celtic or Anglo-Saxon tribes that settled in England hundreds, or even thousands, of years ago.

Many English families live in cities and suburbs such as Leeds.

More and more English classrooms include children from Asia and the West Indies.

The fastest-growing groups of people in England are ethnic minorities, especially blacks and Asians. Most are **immigrants** from countries that were once part of the British Empire in Asia and the West Indies.

Today, most people in England live in large, sprawling cities and their suburbs.

These sleek Eurostar trains at Waterloo Station, London, take passengers through the Chunnel to France and the rest of Europe.

Question What is the Chunnel?

The Channel Tunnel, or Chunnel, is a tunnel underneath the English Channel. It connects England to France and the mainland of Europe. The Chunnel is 31 miles (50 kilometers) long. More than two-thirds of the Chunnel is 150 feet (46 meters) below the ocean floor!

It cost more than $15 billion to build the Chunnel. Almost thirteen thousand engineers, workers, and technicians were used to dig three separate tunnels. It takes passengers on the Eurostar train approximately twenty minutes to pass through the Chunnel.

The Archbishop of Canterbury is the spiritual head of the Church of England.

Winchester Cathedral

People in England enjoy religious freedom, but most belong to the Church of England (Anglican Church). Because England's ruler is known as the Defender of the Faith, every king or queen of England has to be a member of the Anglican Church. Winchester Cathedral, in the city of Winchester, is one of the most beautiful Anglican churches in the world.

The Roman Catholic Church also has a significant number of members in England, and there are many Presbyterians, Methodists, and Baptists as well. England is the home of Europe's second-largest population of Jewish people.

Religion

Library research is a familiar part of life for students throughout the world.

School & Sports

Children in England are required to attend school between the ages of five and sixteen. Many schools are **segregated** by gender. Most English students wear uniforms to classes.

Soccer, known as football in England, is by far the country's most popular sport. David Beckham, an outstanding player who used to play for Manchester United, now plays for Real Madrid. He is still a national hero to many. English soccer fans are very enthusiastic about their favorite teams. Sometimes violence and riots erupt between opposing fans.

Though David Beckham no longer plays for England, he is still enormously popular.

Transportation

England has a modern transportation system. Large trucks carry most of the nation's freight. London is famous for its black taxis, double-decker buses, and underground rail system.

The country's air transportation system is first-class. Working together, the British and French developed the Concorde airplane. It was the world's first commercial, **supersonic** passenger jet. Heathrow Airport in London handles the largest number of international passengers in the world.

Tube

Tube means "underground rail system."

Lorry

Lorry means "truck."

Stonehenge

Unusual Places

Stonehenge is one of the most amazing archeological sites in the world. Original construction may have started as far back as five thousand years ago. A large stone circle is found at the center of the site. The sandstone rocks that make up the circle can weigh up to 50 tons each.

No one knows for sure who built Stonehenge. Some people believe that it was used as a religious ceremonial site. The mysteries of Stonehenge attract almost 1 million tourists each year.

ENTRY TO THE TRAITORS GATE

The Tower of London has been a palace, a fortress, and a prison for nearly one thousand years. Today, it is a popular museum and tourist attraction.

Visiting the Country

No visit to England would be complete without a stop at the Tower of London. The tower once served as a major prison. It was the location of many executions. Two of King Henry VIII's six wives, Anne Boleyn and Catherine Howard, were beheaded there.

Today, the tower is a museum that contains the British Crown Jewels. The Crown Jewels include the Great Star of Africa, which is the world's largest cut diamond. The tower is protected by the **Beefeater Guards.**

Window to the Past

England has been ruled
by kings and queens
for hundreds of years.
William I (William the
Conqueror) claimed
the throne in 1066.

Queen Victoria ruled England for more than sixty years.

Henry VIII was a powerful king in the 1500s. He was responsible for separating the Church of England from the Roman Catholic Church.

Queen Victoria became the ruling monarch in 1837, when she was just eighteen years old. She ruled until 1901. During her reign, the British Empire spread to include a fifth of the world's land and a quarter of the world's people. With Victoria as queen, Britain became the world's richest country!

Queen Elizabeth II is the current ruler. She is very popular with the public.

X-tra Special Things

Hever Castle is protected by a drawbridge.

Moats, like this one around Leeds Castle, offered protection against enemy armies.

Windsor Castle

Castles are a special part of England's history and landscape. Most of England's castles were built during the Middle Ages, a time approximately between the 400s and the 1500s.

Feudal lords built castles to protect their people. The stone fortresses were symbols of a ruler's power and wealth. The invention of gunpowder and artillery led to the destruction of most castles.

Windsor Castle outside of London has been a palace and fortress for at least nine hundred years. It is the largest occupied castle in the world. It serves as one of the official homes of Queen Elizabeth II.

Yearly Festivals

The English observe many of the same holidays that are celebrated in other parts of the world. All Hallows' Eve (Halloween) is the night of October 31. It was originally a Celtic festival to honor the fall harvest. In some cities, it is called Mischief Night. Children dress in costumes and play tricks on their neighbors.

Even adults dress up for Guy Fawkes Night parades.

Fireworks are a popular part of Guy Fawkes Night celebrations.

Some holidays are unique to England. November 5 is Bonfire Night or Guy Fawkes Night. On that date in 1605, a man named Guy Fawkes tried to blow up the Parliament. He wanted to kill King James I, but he failed. This holiday celebrates his failure.

37

The rocky coastline of southwestern England has caused many shipwrecks over the years.

Zantman's Rock

Zantman's Rock is an **exposed** rock outcrop in the Atlantic Ocean. It is located 34 miles (55 km) off the southwestern tip of England.

Zantman's Rock is difficult to see above the ocean's waves. This has caused several shipwrecks. On August 14, 1913, a ship called the *Susanna* hit the rock. Its twenty-two crew members reached safety just before the ship broke in half. The wreck now lies on the ocean floor.

English Words

Beefeater Guards a military unit established in 1485 to protect King Henry VII, whose responsibility today is to guard the Tower of London and the Crown Jewels

blitz an aerial bombing campaign

constitutional monarchy a type of government in which the king or queen has only those powers given by the constitution and laws of the nation, and where elected officials make most political decisions

cunning very clever or good at fooling others

descendants people who come from a particular ancestor or group

exposed left open or revealed

feudal lords wealthy men who owned large plots of land and controlled many workers during the Middle Ages

heirloom an object that is handed down from generation to generation

immigrants people who come to a new country to live

monarch a ruler, such as a king or queen, who often inherits his or her position

moors wild-looking open areas of wet, marshy ground

predators animals who live by hunting other animals

reserves areas of land set aside for special use

segregated separated by race or sex

supersonic moving faster than the speed of sound, which is about 750 miles (1,207 km) per hour

tunics articles of clothing that look like shirts and reach to the knees

Let's Explore More

The Children's Shakespeare by Edith Nesbit, Academy Chicago Publishers, 2000

Fairy Tales from England (Oxford Story Collections) by James Reeves and Rosamund Fowler, Oxford University Press, 1999

Life in a Medieval Castle (English Heritage Series) by Tony McAleavy, Kate Jeffrey, and Brian Davison, Enchanted Lion Books, 2003

Websites

http://www.surfnetkids.com/monarchy.htm
This Surfing the Net with Kids Web site is chock-full of information about the British monarchy. It contains historical data, information on their residences, an ABC glossary of royal vocabulary, and much more.

http://www.woodlands-junior.kent.sch.uk/customs/questions/
This is a wonderful site for elementary students to study English life, culture, and customs. It was prepared by children who live in England and covers almost every topic imaginable.

■ Index

Italic page numbers indicate illustrations.

Meet the Authors

BYRON AND REBECCA AUGUSTIN have been working as an educational team since 1991. They have conducted social studies workshops in several states, as well as the nation's capital. The Augustins have served as consultants for the National Geographic Society, the Texas Alliance for Geographic Education, the National Council on U.S.-Arab Relations, and a host of public school districts.

Byron is a professor of geography at Texas State University–San Marcos. He is a widely published photographer and author. His research travels have taken him to fifty-four countries on five different continents.

Rebecca is an award-winning teacher at Seele Elementary School in New Braunfels, Texas. She has taught several different elementary grade levels. In addition, she served on the faculty of the Department of Education at Northwest Missouri State University and Buena Vista College in Iowa. She has co-authored books with her husband and also published several photos from the Middle East.

A to Z

Take a trip to countries all over the world. Roam with the **A**nimals, see the **B**uildings, tour the **C**ities—cross-cultural comparisons are easy and fun. For a while, you'll live in another land, tasting the **F**ood, learning the **H**istory, meeting the **P**eople, and discovering **X**-tra special things that happen only there. Don't forget to bring back **K**eepsakes to remind you of your travels.

Read other titles in this series:

children's press®
an imprint of
■SCHOLASTIC

www.scholastic.com/librarypublishing

U.S. $6.95

ISBN 0-516-24952-5

9 780516 249520

THE
EVERYTHING
KIDS'
SCRATCH
CODING
BOOK

LEARN TO CODE AND CREATE YOUR OWN COOL GAMES!

JASON RUKMAN